JE - - '14

THE
Washington
Monument

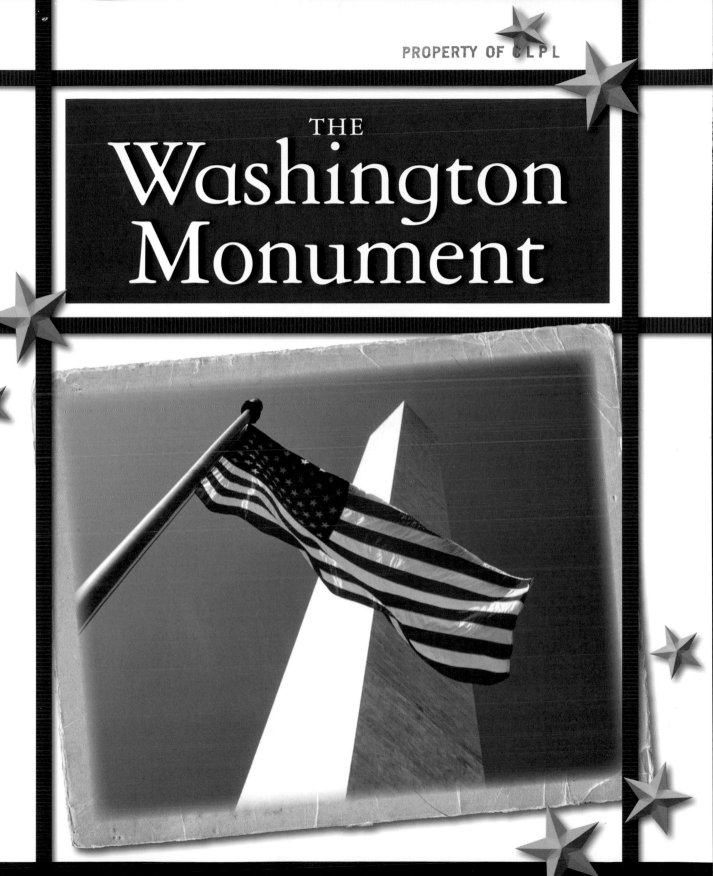

BY FREDERIC GILMORE

Published by The Child's World®
1980 Lookout Drive • Mankato, MN 56003-1705
800-599-READ • www.childsworld.com

Acknowledgments
The Child's World®: Mary Berendes, Publishing Director
The Design Lab: Design
Jody Jensen Shaffer: Editing
Red Line Editorial: Photo Research

Photo credits
Brand X Pictures, cover, 21; Robert King/Library of Congress, 5;
Public Domain, 6; AP Images, 10; Library of Congress, 9, 14;
Buyenlarge/Getty Images, 13; National Park Service, 17; U.S.
Army Corps of Engineers, 18

ISBN 9781623239596
LCCN 2013947398

Printed in the United States of America
Mankato, MN
November, 2013
PA02189

ABOUT THE AUTHOR

*Frederic Gilmore enjoys traveling,
reading, playing games with his wife,
and wrestling with his five children.
He and his family live in Eagan,
Minnesota.*

TABLE OF CONTENTS

★ ★ ★

A City Named Washington

★ ★ ★

In 1789, George Washington became the first President of the United States. He saw a need for a capital city to house the new nation's government. In 1791, a site for the new city was chosen: it would be on the banks of the Potomac River. The capital city was to be called "Washington," after the president. The location of the city would be called "The District of Columbia," after the explorer Christopher Columbus.

A Frenchman named Pierre Charles L'Enfant was hired to design the city. His plan called for a capitol building, a presidential palace, and a large **mall** lined with all the offices of government. Along with all of these buildings, the plan called for a huge monument to honor the achievements of George Washington.

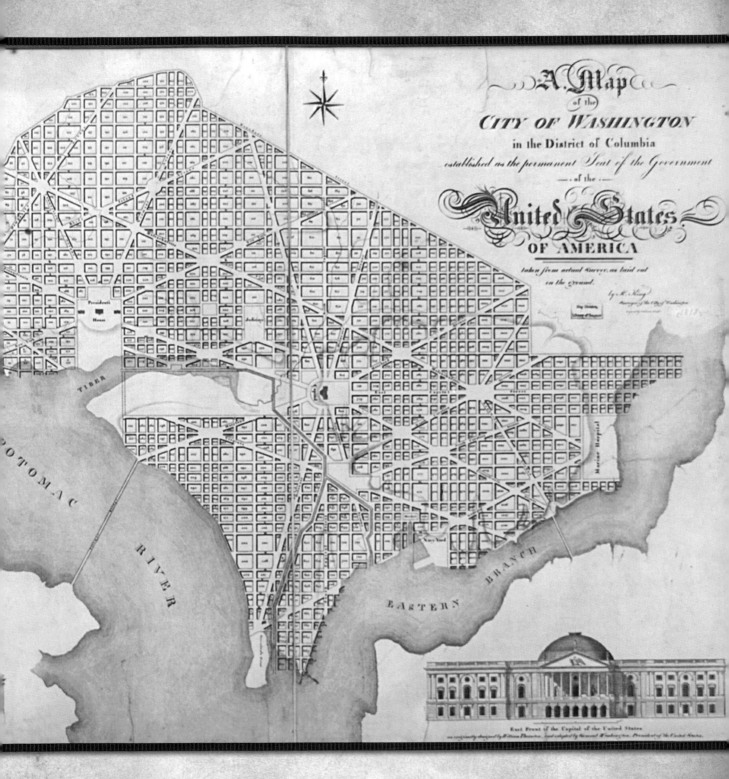

This map shows Washington, D.C., in 1818.

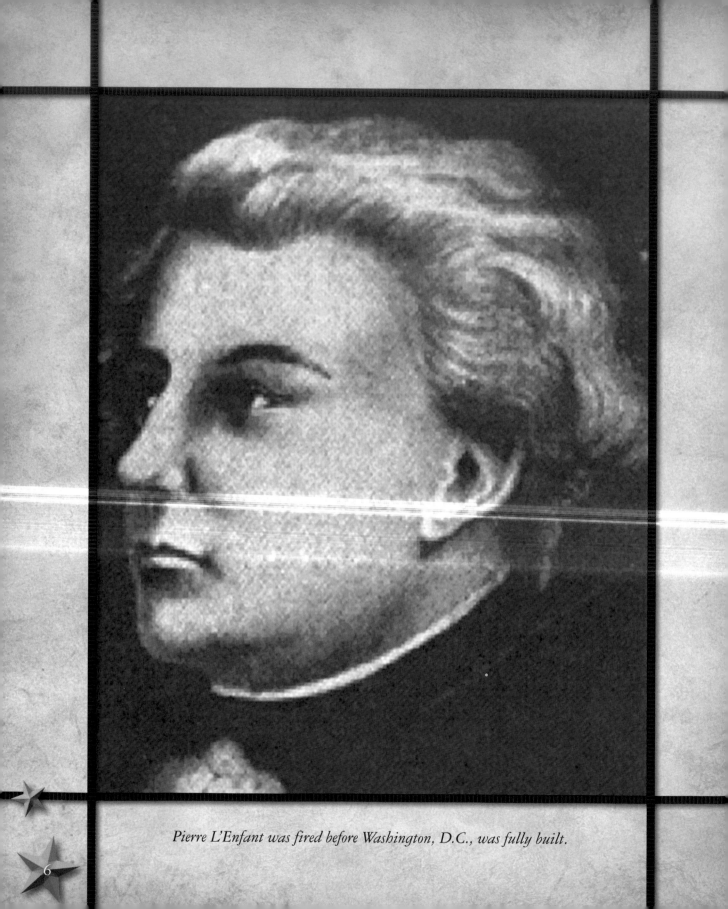

Pierre L'Enfant was fired before Washington, D.C., was fully built.

No Monument for Washington

★ ★ ★

Work began on the new capital city in 1791. Three members of the new government's **Continental Congress** were chosen to oversee the construction. The congressmen and L'Enfant had many disagreements during the construction. Because of the disagreements, L'Enfant was fired in 1792. As a result, the plans for the capital city began to change.

Despite the changes, the plans for the city still included a monument to President Washington. The Congress had considered several ideas for the monument, but no one could agree on what it should look like or how big it should be. Work on the capital city continued, but debates about the monument went on for more than 40 years.

A Plan for a Monument

★ ★ ★

By 1833, Washington, D.C., still did not have
a monument honoring the first president. The
government could not agree on a plan. A group of
people living in the area decided to come up with
a plan of their own. The group called itself the
Washington National Monument Society.

Congress gave the Society permission to collect
money for the monument's construction. Although
many Americans believed a monument should be
built, few people had money to donate. Collecting
enough money for a monument would take years.

As money was being collected, the members of
the Washington National Monument Society began
to look at plans. Robert Mills was a well-known
architect at the time. He presented a plan that was
based on L'Enfant's original idea for the monument.

This is Mills's early idea for the monument.
You can see the large building at the base.

The cornerstone was laid on July 4, 1848.

Mills's plan was for an **elaborate** circular building 100 feet (30 meters) tall and 250 feet (76 meters) across. An **obelisk** tower 500 feet (152 meters) tall would stand on top of the building. It would be so tall that it could be seen from anywhere in Washington, D.C. The Society was so impressed with Mills's idea, they accepted his plan.

The Society now faced another problem—they had collected only $87,000. With so little money, the Society had to eliminate the circular building. They decided to build just the obelisk tower instead.

The base for the huge tower was built 36 feet (11 meters) down into the ground. The **cornerstone** of the building was put in place on July 4, 1848. The outside of the building was built with white **marble** from Maryland. The bottom of the building was a square more than 55 feet (17 meters) long on each side. The walls were 15 feet (about 5 meters) thick.

A Monument Unfinished

★ ★ ★

By 1854, work on the monument was going well, and the obelisk tower was 150 feet (about 46 meters) tall. Then a group called the **Know-Nothing Party** became the main influence to the Washington National Monument Society. The Know-Nothing Party had ideas that were not popular with the public.

Around the same time, a special piece of black marble **donated** by Pope Pius IX was stolen. Pope Pius IX had given the marble to be part of the decoration inside the monument. Many people believed that the Know-Nothing Party was responsible for the missing marble. Also during this time, problems began to arise between the northern and southern states. For all of these reasons, people stopped donating money to the Society. Work on the monument slowly came to a stop.

This photo of the Washington Monument was taken while work was stopped during the Civil War.

The Washington Monument as it was being built.

At just over 150 feet (about 46 meters) tall, the monument to George Washington stood unfinished for years. By 1876, President Ulysses S. Grant grew unhappy that the monument was not finished. Grant asked the members of the Washington National Monument Society to give the unfinished building to the people of the United States. The Society agreed to Grant's request. This made it possible for the federal government to pay for work done on the monument. Now the construction could continue.

A New Beginning

★ ★ ★

On August 2, 1878, work began again on the monument. The Army Corps of Engineers was put in charge of the construction, and the monument began to grow. But the years of no construction had left a mark on the monument. Even though the white marble now being used was from the same **quarry** in Maryland, it was a little darker in color. Today, you can see a ring on the monument about 150 feet (about 46 meters) above the ground where the two colors of marble meet.

Inside the monument, workers built a stairway to a viewing floor at the top. The stairway has 898 steps. "Memorial Stones" were built into the walls of the stairway. The stones were gifts from states as well as from people, organizations, and other nations around the world. The idea of the "Memorial Stones" was similar to the black marble stone donated by Pope Pius IX.

This "Memorial Stone" was given to the monument by the state of New York.

This drawing shows the project superintendent
placing the apex on the monument.

Construction of the monument continued until December 6, 1884. On that date, workers placed an aluminum **apex** on the top of the building, completing the monument. At 555 feet, 5 1/8 inches (a little more than 169 meters) high, the Washington Monument is the tallest **masonry** tower in the world.

A law was passed to keep people from building anything taller than 13 stories in Washington, DC. This meant that no other building in the city would ever be as tall as the Washington Monument. The monument would always be able to be seen as the tallest building in the city.

A Monument to Washington

★ ★ ★

On February 22, 1885, President Chester A. Arthur held a ceremony to open the Washington Monument. In 1888, the monument was opened to the public. A circle of 50 American flags now surrounds the base of the monument. This circle is similar to Mills's original idea for the building.

In the years since, the Washington Monument has been the site of celebrations and ceremonies. It has also been the site of protests and rallies by groups of people expressing their views to our government.

The Washington Monument has become what Pierre L'Enfant had hoped it would be. It is a monument to the great leader George Washington, and it is a widely recognized symbol of the capital of the United States of America.

Here you can see the flags that surround the base of the monument.

Glossary

apex (AY-peks) An apex is the top of an object that comes to a single point. An aluminum apex sits atop the Washington Monument.

Continental Congress (kon-tih-NEN-tull KON-gress) The Continental Congress was the early form of the U.S. government.

cornerstone (KORN-er-stone) A cornerstone is a stone that celebrates the official beginning of a new building project. The Washington Monument's cornerstone was placed in 1848.

donated (DOH-nay-ted) When something is donated, it is given as a gift. Pope Pius IX donated a special stone to the Washington Monument.

elaborate (ee-LAB-ur-et) Something that is elaborate is very decorated or complex. Original plans for the Washington Monument called for a very elaborate building.

Know-Nothing Party (NO NUTH-ing PAR-tee) The Know-Nothing Party was a group of people in the 1800s who did not like newcomers or Catholics in America. Some people blamed the Know-Nothing Party for the disappearance of a special stone given by Pope Pius IX, the head of the Catholic Church.

mall (MALL) A mall is large, public area where people can walk. L'Enfant's city plan called for a large mall.

marble (MAR-bull) Marble is a type of stone that is very hard and good for building. The Washington Monument is made of marble.

masonry (MAY-sun-ree) Masonry is building with stones, bricks, or blocks. The Washington Monument is a masonry tower.

obelisk (OB-uh-lisk) An obelisk is a four-sided tower that gets smaller as it gets taller and has a point on top. The Washington Monument is an obelisk building.

Find Out More

IN THE LIBRARY

Ashabranner, Brent. *The Washington Monument: A Beacon for America.* Brookfield, CT: Twenty-First Century Books, 2002.

Landau, Elaine. *The Washington Monument.* New York: Children's Press, 2009.

Linde, Barbara M. *Building Washington, D.C: Measuring the Area of Rectangular Spaces.* New York: PowerKids Press, 2004.

Schaffer, Julia. *The Washington Monument.* New York: Chelsea Clubhouse, 2010.

ON THE WEB

Visit our Web site for lots of links about the Washington Monument: *www.childsworld.com/links*

Note to Parents, Teachers, and Librarians: We routinely check our Web links to make sure they're safe, active sites—so encourage your readers to check them out!

Index